CONTENTS

Words that appear in the text in bold, **like this**, are explained in the Glossary.

WHAT IS A CONTINENT?

About two-thirds of the Earth is covered in water. The rest of the Earth is made up of seven huge pieces of land, called continents. Each of the continents, apart from Antarctica, is divided up into smaller regions called countries. This book is about the continent of Asia.

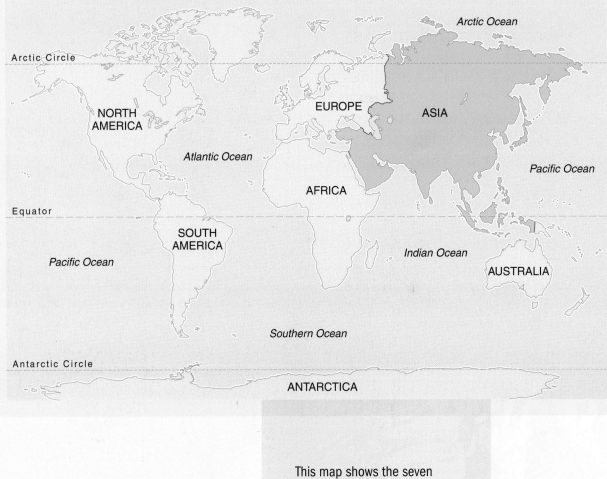

This map shows the seven continents of the world.

EXPLORING CONTINENTS

ASIA

Anita Ganeri

Heinemann
LIBRARY

H www.heinemann.co.uk/library
Visit our website to find out more information about Heinemann Library books.

To order:
☎ Phone 44 (0) 1865 888066
🖹 Send a fax to 44 (0) 1865 314091
💻 Visit the Heinemann Bookshop at www.heinemann.co.uk/library to browse our catalogue and order online.

First published in Great Britain by Heinemann, Halley Court, Jordan Hill, Oxford, OX2 8EJ, part of Harcourt Education.

© Harcourt Education Ltd 2007
First published in paperback in 2008
The moral right of the proprietor has been asserted.

Editorial: Louise Galpine and Harriet Milles
Design: Richard Parker and Q2A Solutions
Illustrations: Jeff Edwards
Picture Research: Mica Brancic and Beatrice Ray
Production: Camilla Crask

Originated by Chroma
Printed and bound in China by WKT

13 digit ISBN 978 0 431 09744 2 (hardback)
11 10 09 08 07
10 9 8 7 6 5 4 3 2 1

13 digit ISBN 978 0 431 09752 7 (paperback)
12 11 10 09 08
10 9 8 7 6 5 4 3 2 1

British Library Cataloguing in Publication Data
Ganeri, Anita
Asia. - (Exploring continents)
1. Asia - Geography - Juvenile literature
I.Title
915
A full catalogue record for this book is available from the British Library.

Acknowledgements
Alamy pp. **8** (Danita Delimont), **9** (Viewstock China), **10** (Alan Compton), **14** (Stefan Auth), **16** (Denis Fast), **25** (James Gritz); Corbis pp. **13** (Frans Lanting), **15** (Theo Allofs), **18** (Bojan Brecelj), **24** (Richard T Nowitz), **27** (Jose Fuste Raga); Getty pp. **5** (Stone), **11** (National Geographic), **21** (Asia Images), **22** (Photonica), **23** (Stone); Superstock p. **19**; Travel Ink p. **7**.

Cover satellite image of Asia reproduced with permission of SPL/M-Sat Ltd.

Every effort has been made to contact copyright holders of any material reproduced in this book. Any omissions will be rectified in subsequent printings if notice is given to the publishers.

How big is Asia?

Asia is the world's largest continent. It covers almost a third of the Earth's land surface. It stretches from Africa and Europe in the west, to the Pacific Ocean in the east. The northern part of Asia lies in the icy Arctic. But Asia stretches southwards to the hot, steamy places around the **equator.** Because of its vast size, Asia has a wide range of **climates** and landscapes.

Islands and coasts

Thousands of islands form part of Asia. These islands include Sri Lanka, most of Indonesia, the Philippines, and Japan. The whole of Asia's coastline measures about 130,000 kilometres (80,778 miles). If it could be stretched out, it would be long enough to reach three times around the equator.

Indonesia is the world's largest **archipelago** (group of islands). It is made up of more than 13,600 islands, but people only live on about 6,000 of them.

WHAT DOES ASIA LOOK LIKE?

Asia is so enormous that it has almost every type of landscape. It has some of the world's driest deserts, longest rivers, largest lakes, and biggest forests. The highest (Mount Everest) and lowest (Dead Sea) points on Earth are both in Asia.

Record-breaking mountains

Many of the world's greatest mountains are found in the continent of Asia. In the west, the Ural Mountains in Russia divide Asia and Europe. The Pamir Mountains in Central Asia rise over 7,500 metres (24,606 ft).

This map shows some of the dramatic natural features found in Asia.

Hundreds of climbers have died in their attempts to reach the summit of Mount Everest.

On top of the world

The most famous mountains in Asia are the Himalayas to the north of India and Nepal. The Himalayas are the highest mountain range on Earth, with nine out of ten of the world's highest peaks.

At 8,850 metres (29,035 feet), Mount Everest in the Himalayas is the world's highest mountain. The first people to reach the top of Everest were the Nepalese climber, Tenzing Norgay, and New Zealander, Edmund Hillary, in May 1953.

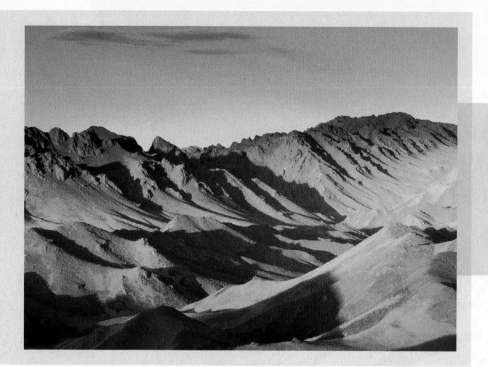

The Gobi Desert stretches along the border between China and Mongolia.

Spreading deserts

Large parts of western and central Asia are covered by desert. The Arabian Desert in Saudi Arabia contains the Rub al Khali, or Empty Quarter, a huge sandy desert which covers an area of 650,000 square kilometres (250,965 square miles). The Kyzlkum Desert stretches across Kazakhstan and Uzbekistan. The Karakum covers most of Turkmenistan. The Thar Desert lies across the border of India and Pakistan. Further east lies the Takla Makan Desert in China.

Large lakes

Asia has many large lakes. The largest lake in the world is the Caspian Sea. It covers 371,000 square kilometres (143,250 square miles) and lies partly in Azerbaijan, Iran, Turkmenistan, Kazakhstan, and Russia. This enormous lake is called a sea because it is filled with salt water.

Lake Baikal in Siberia is the deepest lake on Earth. It is up to 1,620 metres (5,315 feet) deep. It is famous for its wildlife, including the world's only freshwater seal.

Raging rivers

The Tigris and Euphrates rivers flow from Turkey across Iraq. The world's first **civilizations** grew up on the rich farmland between these two rivers. The River Ganges flows from the Himalayas across northern India to the Bay of Bengal, in India and Bangladesh. There it joins the Brahmaputra River to form the world's largest river **delta**.

The Yangtze River in China is the longest river in Asia and the third longest river on Earth.

Did you know?

The Dead Sea in Israel and Jordan is the lowest place on Earth. It is 400 metres (1,312 feet) below sea level. Like the Caspian Sea, the Dead Sea is a saltwater lake. It got its name because its water is so salty that almost nothing can live in it.

WHAT IS THE WEATHER LIKE IN ASIA?

Asia is such a big place that is has a wide range of climates. In the far north, the weather is bitterly cold. On the deserts and plains in the centre of the continent, almost no rain falls. They are some of the driest places on Earth. In the south of Asia, around the equator, the weather is hot and sticky all year round.

Monsoons

Winds called monsoons play an important part in Asia's weather. In summer, these winds bring very heavy rain to places like India and Sri Lanka. Farmers rely on this rain to water their fields. If there is not enough rain, their crops will be spoilt. But if the rain is too heavy, it can flood their fields.

The monsoon rains can flood cities and force people to leave their homes.

Reindeer find very little to eat on the frozen Siberian **tundra**.

Frozen ground

Siberia is part of Russia. It lies in the far north of Asia. This vast region stretches from the Ural Mountains in the west right across to the Pacific Ocean in the east. In the far north of Siberia, the climate is so cold that the top layers of the ground stay frozen all year round. Very few plants can survive here.

Wild weather

Each year, some parts of Asia are hit by tropical storms called **typhoons.** These storms bring winds travelling at over 200 kilometres (125 miles) per hour, and can kill people and destroy buildings. The places most at risk are along the coast. These are low-lying so they are easily flooded by the high waves whipped up by the winds.

ASIA'S WEATHER FACTS

◉ *Highest recorded temperature:* Tirat Tsvi, Israel: 53.8°C (129°F)

◉ *Lowest recorded temperature:* Oimekon and Verkhoyansk in Russia: minus 67.8°C (minus 90°F)

◉ *Highest average rainfall:* Mawsynram, India: 11,872 mm (467.4 inches) per year

◉ *Lowest average rainfall:* Aden, Yemen: 46 mm (1.8 inches) per year

WHAT PLANTS AND ANIMALS LIVE IN ASIA?

Asia has a wide range of **habitats**, from mountains to deserts to rainforests. These habitats provide homes to an amazing number of plants and animals.

Northern forest

The largest forest in the world stretches across Siberia. The trees in the forest are **coniferous**, which means that most of them do not lose their leaves in winter. They are well **adapted** to the cold Siberian weather. Their leaves are needle-shaped so that they do not lose too much water and dry out. Their branches bend easily so that heavy snow can slide off without snapping them.

This map shows the range of different kinds of plants that can be found in Asia.

Arctic Ocean

Ural Mts.

Gobi Desert

Himalayas

Pacific Ocean

Indian Ocean

0   1000 miles
0   1000 km

N
W—E
S

Tropical rainforest
Monsoon woodland and jungle
Subtropical and temperate rainforest
Evergreen trees and shrubs
Broad-leaved forest and meadow
Coniferous forest
Grassland
Steppe and semidesert
Desert
Alpine, tundra and high plateau

Mangrove swamps

Further south muddy mangrove swamps grow along some coasts where rivers flow into the sea. There are large swamps around the Bay of Bengal in India and Bangladesh, and in the Philippines, Thailand, and Indonesia. The swamps are filled with mangrove trees. These trees have two types of roots. Some roots fix the trees firmly in the mud to stop the tides washing them away. Other roots stick out of the water. They take in air for the trees.

Near the equator, the climate is warm and sticky all year round. Tropical rainforests grow here. Many valuable products, such as rubber, wood, spices, and medicines, come from rainforest plants.

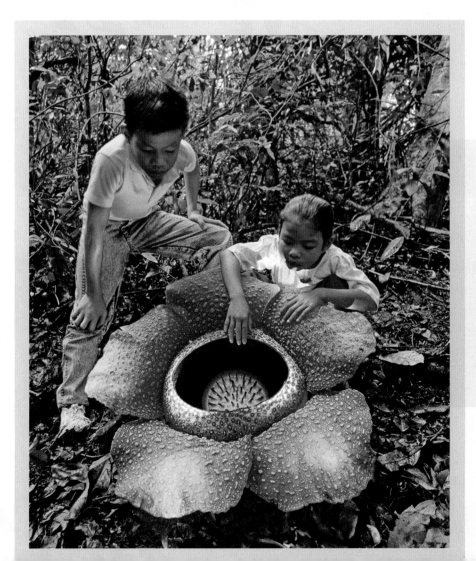

The rafflesia is a plant that has the world's largest flower. It measures up to 1 metre (just over 3 feet) across. It grows in the rainforests of Borneo and Sumatra in South East Asia. Its enormous orange-brown flower smells of rotting meat!

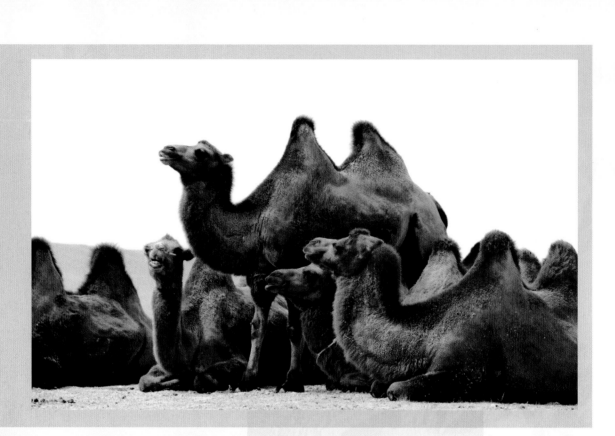

Camels are perfectly adapted for living in the desert. They can store fat in their bodies for food.

Life in the desert

It is difficult for animals to live in Asia's deserts because the deserts are so hot and dry. Even so, many animals have adapted to desert life. Camels can go for days without drinking water. They have big, flat feet for walking over sand and can close their nostrils to keep sand out.

Many small desert animals spend the day underground in their burrows, sheltering from the heat. They come out at night when it is cooler. Jerboas are small furry animals that live in the deserts of Asia. They always walk upright and can hop faster than a person can run.

Mountain animals

Mountains, such as the Himalayas, have many different places for animals to live. Bears live in the forests that cover the bottom of the mountain slopes. Higher up, where it is colder and windier, animals such as yaks, snow leopards, and antelopes live. Vultures fly above the mountain slopes, looking for dead animals to eat.

Animals in danger

Many of the animals that live in Asia's forests are in danger of dying out because their wild homes are being destroyed. Giant pandas live in the mountain forests of south-west China. They feed mainly on **bamboo**. As the forests are cut down to make farmland, so the pandas are losing their supply of food.

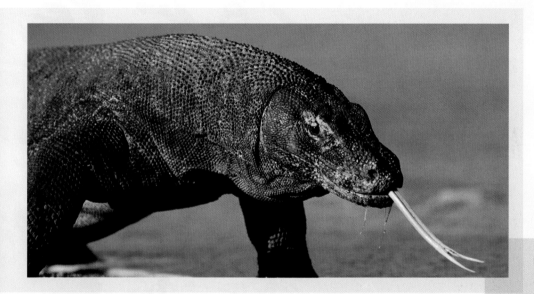

The Komodo dragon's tongue picks up scents to help it find food.

Did you know?

The Komodo dragon is the world's largest lizard. It can grow up to 3 metres (almost 10 feet) long. It lives only on Komodo and a few other islands in Indonesia. The dragon eats wild pigs, deer, and goats, which it swallows whole.

Arctic animals

Animals that live in freezing Siberia have to be tough to survive. But they have special features to help them. The snowy owl has thick feathers to keep it warm. Its feathers have black and white speckles. The colour and pattern help to hide the owl against the snow as it hunts for voles and other small animals to eat.

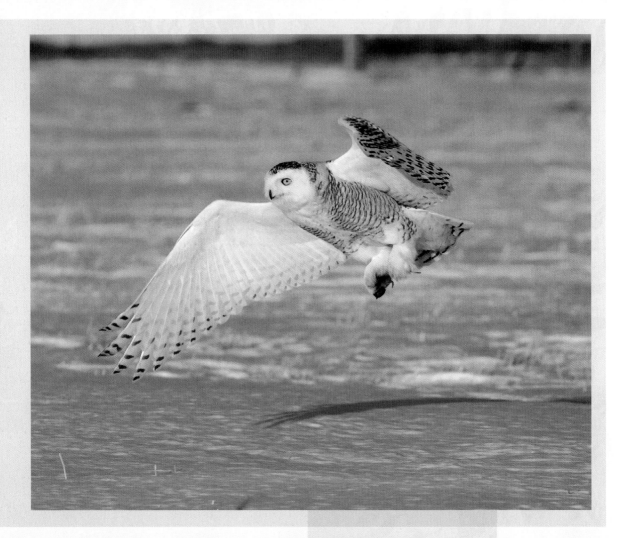

The snowy owl has to have extremely good eyesight to hunt in this difficult terrain.

WHAT ARE ASIA'S NATURAL RESOURCES?

Asia has many **natural resources**. Some countries, such as Saudi Arabia, Japan, and China, have used their natural resources to build up strong industries. This has helped them to become rich. But many countries, such as Bangladesh and Nepal, have not developed so quickly. They are still very poor. People in these countries mainly work as farmers.

Useful resources

The Middle East in south-west Asia produces a lot of the world's oil. Before oil was discovered, the countries in the Middle East were quite poor. But selling oil has made them very rich. Oil and gas also come from the tiny country of Brunei in southeast Asia. Malaysia produces large amounts of **palm oil** and rubber. Myanmar and Sri Lanka are famous for their gemstones, including sapphires and rubies.

Crops
- ☞ Coffee
- 🍃 Cotton
- 🍋 Fruit
- 🌾 Millet
- ⋎ Rice
- 🟫 Rubber
- 🍂 Soya
- ⬚ Sugar
- ⚘ Tea
- 丷 Wheat

Mining
- ✕ Minerals and ores

Power
- ⛏ Coal
- ◗ Gas
- ⬛ Oil

Industry
- ⤳ Fishing
- 🌲 Forestry
- ▢ High-tech
- ⚒ Manufacturing

Livestock
- 🐄 Cattle
- 🐑 Sheep

This map shows where different natural resources can be found in Asia.

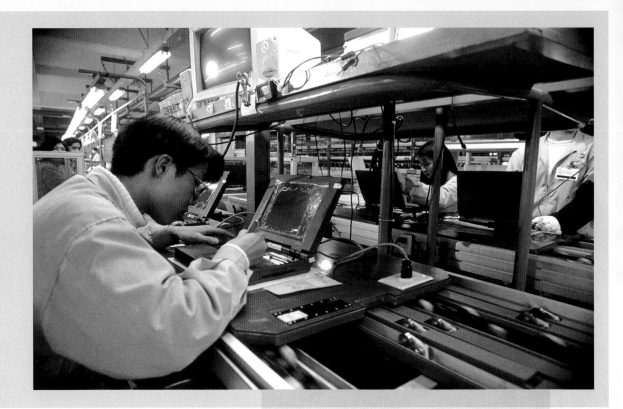

Taiwan is well known for producing many different kinds of electronic goods.

Growing industries

Many Asian countries have important industries. China, India, Japan, Russia, Taiwan, and South Korea have many modern factories. These factories make cars, iron, steel, weapons, ships, and machinery. Japan is one of the top industrial countries in the world. Japanese businesses **export** huge amounts of goods, from cars to computers. Countries, such as China and India, are working hard to build up their industries.

Tourism

Tourism makes a lot of money for many Asian countries. Thousands of tourists from all over the world visit countries such as Thailand, Indonesia, and Sri Lanka. They go to see the breathtaking scenery and beautiful buildings, and to relax on the golden sandy beaches.

Farming

Over half of all the people in Asia earn their living by farming.
In many Asian countries, farmers do not use modern farm machinery.
Their farms are often very small. The farmers struggle to grow
enough crops to feed their families and to sell at market. Some
Asian countries, such as Japan and Israel, have large, modern
farms. They use modern **irrigation** systems to grow large
amounts of crops.

Major crops

The most important crops grown in Asia are rice and wheat. Rice is
the main food for many Asian people. Most of the world's tea and
rubber also comes from Asia. Other crops include cotton, **jute**,
and sugar cane.

Many Asian farmers still use hand tools and animals,
such as water buffalo, to pull their ploughs.

WHAT COUNTRIES AND CITIES ARE IN ASIA?

Asia is divided into 50 countries. Most of these are whole countries, but part of Turkey and part of Russia also lie in Asia. The rest of Turkey and Russia are in Europe. China is the largest country which lies wholly in Asia. It covers 9,597,000 square kilometres (3,705,422 square miles). The smallest country is the tiny island country of the Maldives. It covers just 300 square kilometres (115 square miles).

This map shows all the countries in Asia. It is easy to see how much they vary in size.

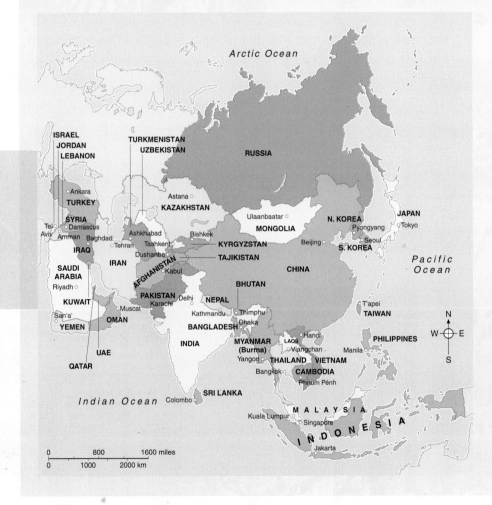

Asian history

Asia has a long history. The world's first civilizations grew up in Asia about 5,500 years ago. They built the world's first cities and farms. People from Asia also invented the first system of writing.

From the 1500s, Europeans came to Asia to trade. They wanted to take the wealth of Asian countries for themselves. European countries, such as Britain, Spain, and France, began to rule countries such as India, the Philippines, and Vietnam. During the 1900s, Asian countries gained their freedom from these foreign rulers.

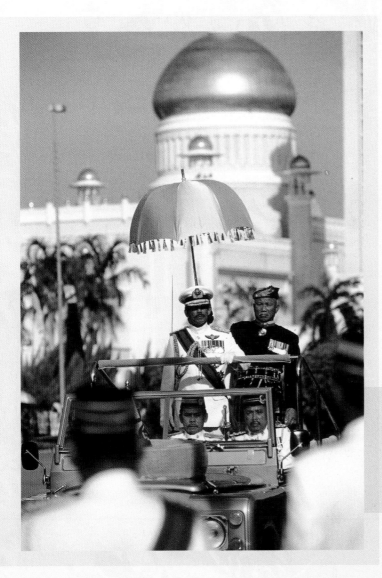

Government and politics

Today, the countries of Asia are governed in many different ways. Bhutan, Saudi Arabia, and Thailand are ruled by kings. Brunei is ruled by a **sultan**. Bahrain and Qatar have leaders called **sheiks**. **Communist governments** rule China, North Korea, and Vietnam. Countries including India, Israel, Mongolia, Japan, and South Korea are **democracies**.

This photograph shows the Sultan of Brunei in the grounds of his palace.

21

Cities of Asia

Asia's cities are growing very fast. This is because many poor people are moving from the countryside into the cities to search for work. Many cities now have more than 10 million people living in them. The largest cities on the continent are Mumbai in India (13 million people), Seoul in South Korea (12 million people), and Karachi in Pakistan (11 million people).

Did you know?

Istanbul (above) in Turkey is the only city in the world that is split between two continents. Part of it lies in Asia and part in Europe. The two parts of the city are separated by a narrow stretch of water, called the Bosphorus. Istanbul is the largest city in Turkey.

WHO LIVES IN ASIA?

Today, almost 4,000 million people live in Asia. This means about three out of every five people on Earth live in Asia. Asia has seven out of ten of the world's most crowded countries. China and India are at the top of the list. Between them, these two countries are home to about 40 per cent of the world's population.

Population figures

Some parts of Asia are very crowded, particularly along the coasts, river valleys, and in the big cities. This is where it is easier for people to grow crops or find jobs. But very few people live in places such as the deserts or the frozen north.

Some cities, like Tokyo in Japan, have become very big and busy. People come to live there to find jobs.

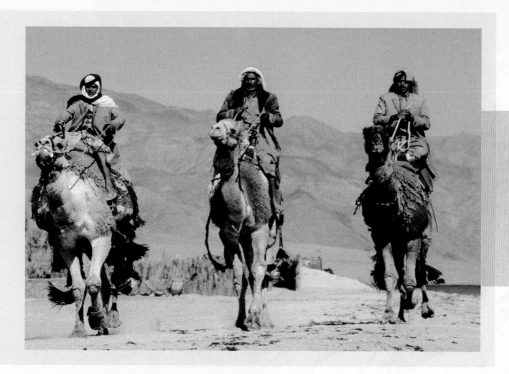

The Bedouin wander through the desert in search of food and water for their animals.

The people of Asia

The people of Asia follow many different ways of life, speak different languages, and have different religious beliefs. In southwest Asia, Arabs are the largest group of people. They speak Arabic and follow the religion of Islam. Some Arabs, called Bedouin, live as **nomads**. The Bedouin live in tents which are light and easy to carry.

In east Asia, Chinese people make up most of the population. Many Chinese people have also settled in other Asian countries, such as Malaysia and Singapore.

Asian languages

Thousands of different languages are spoken in Asia. Many people speak more than one language. Mandarin Chinese is spoken by more people than any other language. More than one **billion** people speak it. Other widely-spoken Asian languages are Hindustani, Arabic, Bengali, and Japanese.

Religions of Asia

All six of the world's main religions began in Asia. They are Buddhism, Christianity, Hinduism, Islam, Judaism, and Sikhism. Religion is still very important in the lives of the people of Asia.

- Hinduism is the main faith in India and Nepal.
- Many people in southwest and central Asia are Muslims who follow Islam.
- Buddhism is followed in southeast Asia and is also widespread in Sri Lanka, Tibet, China, and Japan.
- Judaism is the main religion in Israel.
- Sikhism started in the Punjab, now divided between Pakistan and India.
- Christianity is widespread in the Philippines and parts of Russia.

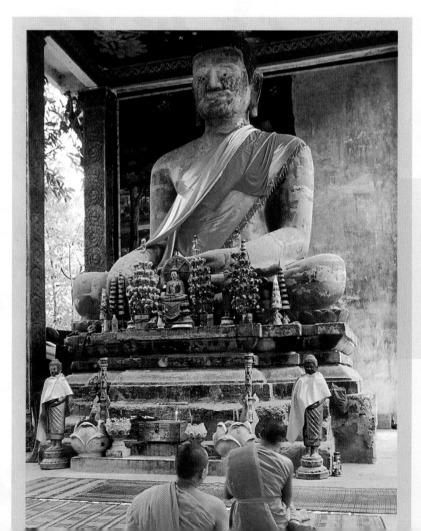

Buddhist monks across Asia pray to statues of the Buddha. These monks are in Cambodia.

WHAT FAMOUS PLACES ARE IN ASIA?

Asia has an amazing number of famous places. They range from natural wonders, to ancient ruins and modern landmarks.

Natural wonders

Asia has many natural wonders. Mount Fuji in Japan is one of the most famous mountains in Asia. It is 3,776 metres (12,388 feet) high. Its perfect cone shape can be seen from miles around. Mount Fuji has become a symbol of Japan.

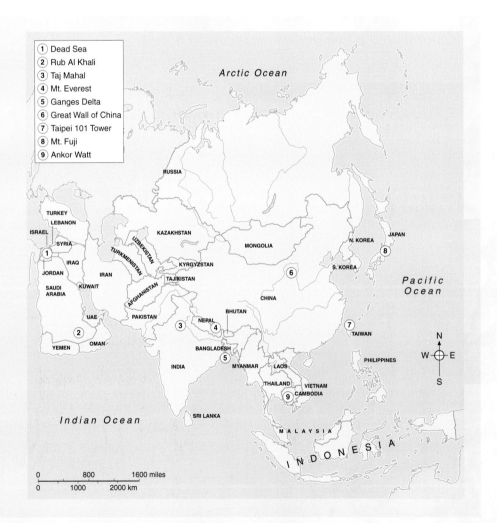

1. Dead Sea
2. Rub Al Khali
3. Taj Mahal
4. Mt. Everest
5. Ganges Delta
6. Great Wall of China
7. Taipei 101 Tower
8. Mt. Fuji
9. Ankor Watt

This map shows some of the amazing wonders found in Asia.

Ancient landmarks

Many ancient buildings are found in Asia. The Great Wall of China stretches for over 7,300 kilometres (4,500 miles) across northern China. It was built over thousands of years, to keep invaders out of the country. It is the only man-made structure that can be seen from space!

The Taj Mahal was built in India in the 1600s by the emperor, Shah Jahan. It was a memorial for his dead wife. It is built from white marble and took over 20 years to finish. The inside of the building is decorated with precious and semi-precious stones.

Modern landmarks

Asia has many modern landmarks and buildings. One of the most striking is the luxurious Burj al Arab hotel in Dubai, in the United Arab Emirates. The TFC 101 Tower in Taipei, Taiwan was built in 2004. It is 508 metres (1,666 feet) high. Super-fast lifts carry passengers to the top of the 91-storey tower in just 30 seconds.

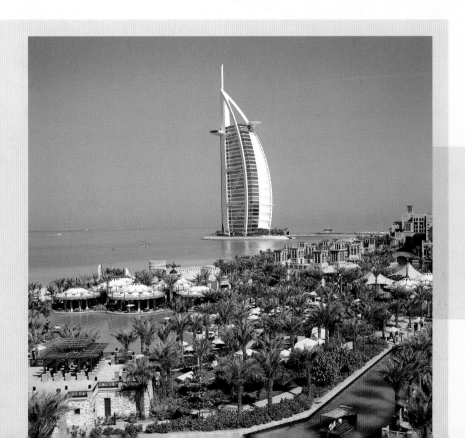

The Burj al Arab hotel overlooks the sea and is shaped like an enormous ship's sail. It was built in 1999.

CONTINENTS COMPARISON CHART

Continent	Area	Population	
AFRICA	30,365,000 square kilometres (11,720,000 square miles)	906 million	
ANTARCTICA	14,200,000 square kilometres (5,500,000 square miles)	officially none, but about 4,000 people live on the research stations during the summer and over 3,000 people visit as tourists each year. People have lived there for as long as three and a half years at a time.	
ASIA	44,614,000 square kilometres (17,226,200 square miles)	almost 4,000 million	
AUSTRALIA	7,713,364 square kilometres (2,966,136 square miles)	approximately 20,090,400 (2005 estimate)	
EUROPE	10,400,000 square kilometres (4,000,000 square miles)	approximately 727 million (2005 estimate)	
NORTH AMERICA	24,230,000 square kilometres (9,355,000 square miles)	approximately 509,915,000 (2005 estimate)	
SOUTH AMERICA	17,814,000 square kilometres (6,878,000 square miles)	380 million	

Number of Countries	Highest Point	Longest River
54 (includes Western Sahara)	Mount Kilimanjaro, Tanzania — 5,895 metres (19,340 feet)	Nile River — 6,695 kilometres (4,160 miles)
none, but over 23 countries have research stations in Antarctica	Vinson Massif — 4,897 metres (16,067 feet)	River Onyx — 12 kilometres (7.5 miles) **Biggest Ice Shelf** Ross Ice Shelf in western Antarctica — 965 kilometres (600 miles) long.
50	Mount Everest, Tibet and Nepal — 8,850 metres (29,035 feet)	Yangtze River, China — 6,300 kilometres (3,914 miles)
1	Mount Kosciusko — 2,229 metres (7,313 feet)	Murray River — 2,520 kilometres (1,566 miles)
47	Mount Elbrus, Russia — 5,642 metres (18,510 feet)	River Volga — 3,685 kilometres (2,290 miles)
23	Mount McKinley (Denali) in Alaska — 6,194 metres (20,320 feet)	Mississippi/Missouri River System — 6,270 kilometres (3,895 miles)
12	Aconcagua, Argentina — 6,959 metres (22,834 feet)	Amazon River — 6,400 kilometres (4,000 miles)

GLOSSARY

adapted when plants or animals have special features to help them live in a place

archipelago group of islands

bamboo tall tropical plant with grassy leaves and thin wooden stems

billion a million million

civilizations ancient peoples and their cultures

climate weather places usually have over a long time

communist government government that owns all their country's land and controls all their people's jobs

coniferous trees which have needles instead of leaves and grow cones. Most conifers do not lose their leaves in winter.

delta land formed from sand and mud where a river flows into the sea

democracy country ruled by a government that has been elected by the people

equator imaginary line around the middle of the Earth

export to sell to other countries

habitat place where plants and animals live

irrigation how water is brought to farmers' fields

jute plant fibres used to make mats, sacks, and ropes

natural resources country's stocks of coal, oil, metals, and so on

nomads people who move from place to place

palm oil oil from palm trees which is used in many products, including bread, chocolate, crisps, and cleaning products

plough piece of farm machinery used for digging up the soil

sheikh chief or leader in the Arab world

sultan title of a Muslim king

tundra flat land where there are few trees and the soil is partly frozen all year

typhoon tropical storm. Also known as hurricane or cyclone.

FURTHER INFORMATION

Books

All About Continents: Africa, Europe & Asia, Bruce McClish (Heinemann Library, 2004)

A World of Recipes: Indonesia, S. Townsend and C. Young (Heinemann Library, 2004)

Continents: Asia, Leila Merrell Foster (Heinemann Library, 2002)

Destination Detectives: Japan, Jen Green (Raintree, 2005)

Settlements of the Ganges River, Richard Spilsbury (Heinemann Library, 2005)

Useful websites

- Lots of facts, figures, statistics, and maps about the world's continents, countries, cities, languages, and people: www.worldatlas.com
- Profiles of Asian countries, details of current events, and information about every aspect of Asian art, religion, culture, and politics: www.askasia.org
- Map-based games based on the countries and capital cities of Asia: www.sheppardsoftware.com/Asian_Geography

Disclaimer

All the internet addresses (URLs) given in this book were valid at the time of going to press. However, due to the dynamic nature of the internet, some addresses may have changed, or sites may have ceased to exist since publication. While the author and publishers regret any inconvenience this may cause readers, no responsibility for such changes can be accepted by either the author(s) or the publishers.

INDEX